Rockin' with the Rules!

CHECK OUT ALL THESE

★ GOLD NUGGET GUIDES ★

★ *Rockin' with the Rules*
Understanding the Ten Commandments

★ *Beyond a Blast From the Past*
Discovering why God made you

★ *More than a Splatball Game*
Squaring off with the giants in your life

God Rocks!

Rockin' with the Rules!

Understanding the
Ten Commandments

Standard
PUBLISHING
CINCINNATI, OHIO

Published by Standard Publishing, Cincinnati, Ohio. A division of Standex International Corporation. Printed in Italy.

Written by Lise Caldwell. Art by Chelsea Road Productions, Inc. Project editor: Robin Stanley. Art direction and design: Rule29. Cover design: Rule29. Production: settingPace.

ISBN 0-7847-1127-5

09 08 07 06 05 04 03   9 8 7 6 5 4 3 2 1

Rockin' with the Rules!

CONTENTS

GOD ROCKS HALL OF FAME

WELCOME TO ROCKY RIDGE . . .

. . . Home of the God Rocks Hall of Fame, where you can see famous rocks from the Bible on display. There's always a new exhibit coming to town, and you never know who you'll bump into! You might meet the five smooth stones David picked up when he went to battle against Goliath, or the stone tablets God gave to Moses with the Ten Commandments on them!

But the interesting rocks aren't all in the Hall of Fame. Rocky Ridge is also home to Chip Livingstone. Chip is your average guy. He likes to play with his dog, Ruff, tease his sister, Nuggie, and, oh yeah, he's in a band called The God Rocks! The God Rocks! is a praise band. Band members know that "If the world won't yell it out, we, the rocks, will cheer and shout! God Rocks! God Rocks!" Along with his friends Gem, Splinter, and Carb, Chip digs writing and rehearsing songs with the band.

Chip's mom and dad, Ruby and Cliff, who think they are just as sparkin' as the younger rocks, look out for Chip and Nuggie and work hard to teach their family about God's love.

Pastor Jasper, the minister of Stone Church, and Mrs. Crag, the teacher at Rocky Ridge Academy, watch out for Chip and his friends. But, as you'll see, they often kick in on the fun, too!

So come along and get to know The God Rocks! and their friends a little better. You'll have a rockin' good time!

AN OVERVIEW OF TEN ROCKIN' RULES!

Chip Livingstone has had it. He is fed up with all the rules! "No rockman music at the breakfast table," his parents say. While he's eating lunch with his friends Gem, Splinter, and Carb, he sees a sign in the cafeteria that declares "No throwing food!" And his teacher, Mrs. Crag, bursts his bubble, literally, when she won't let him chew gum in school. With all these rules, how can a rock kid have any fun?

Things are looking up when his class at Rocky Ridge Academy goes on a field trip to the God Rocks Hall of Fame. But there are rules there, too! In fact, the new exhibit is all *about* rules—God's Rules. When Chip breaks the "do not touch" rule, he gets an idea of what the world would be like with no rules at all. By the time Gem, Splinter, and Carb find him, he's decided that he *wants* to live in a world with rules, after all.

The four friends meet TC and TC 2, the Ten Commandment Twins, who tell them the story of how God's rules were inscribed on these two groovy stones. Mrs. Crag even gets into the act when Chip and his friends—who are The God Rocks! band—sing all about God's Rockin' Rules!

What *do* you do with Rockin' Rules?
Look here and find out!

Crack open the pages of this book and get ready for a rockin' good time, as Chip Livingstone and his friends learn about the Ten Commandments.

God gave his people, the Israelites, the Ten Commandments so they would know how to obey and please God. He did NOT give them rules to take all their fun away. He gave them (and us!) these rules because God knows what is best for us. How? Because he *made* us and he *loves* us.

Each chapter in this book begins with one of the Ten Commandments found in Exodus 20 in the Bible. There's also a story about the God Rocks and how they obey (or not!) the commandment. After each story you'll also find . . .

* Thinkin' It Through—questions to help you think about the main point of the story

* TC Twins Talk Ten—the inside scoop from the rocks who were there

* Set in Stone: TC Twins Memory Verse—a special Bible verse for you to remember

* Get Rockin'—great ideas for you to put the commandment into action, including some space for writing down your thoughts

If you want, you can read a little bit of each chapter every day so you have plenty of time to think about the story, answer the questions, learn the verse, and put the commandment into action. Or read a chapter all at once! Whatever you do, have a great time learning about the rules God gave us for right living.

CHAPTER 1

PRAISE GOD, NOT ROCKS

You shall have no other gods before me. Exodus 20:3

"**L**adies and gentlemen, we are about to witness the final frame of the Rock Bowling World Championships! In what has been an amazing turn of events, an unknown rock from Rocky Ridge, Carb Onate, is about to pull off an upset victory." A hush falls over the crowd as Carb tumbles down the alley toward the bowling pins. Strike! Victory! The crowd goes wild, shouting, "Carb! Carb! Carb . . ."

"Carb! Carb! Can you hear me, rock?" asked his friend Chip as he stood behind him. "You look like you're in another universe."

Carb's dreams of victory melted away. "I was just thinking about bowling. Someday I'm gonna be the best bowling rock in the world!"

"Right now, I'd settle for your being the best drummer in Rocky Ridge. It's time for us to rehearse for our next God Rocks! concert," Chip said. "Gem and Splinter will be here any minute!"

"Rehearsal! I can't rehearse," said Carb. "I've gotta go bowling. Those other bowling rocks at the alley need someone to show them how it's done. Besides, I already know all our songs; I don't need to rehearse!"

He's a good drummer, thought Chip, *but not that good.* Before Chip could say anything, Carb was gone. Chip has been friends with Carb for a long time. Carb has always been a little impulsive but this bowling thing was really hanging on. It was going to be hard to have a band rehearsal without their drummer.

When the rest of The God Rocks! band, Gem and Splinter, got there, they decided they had to do something about Carb. "Rocks, the drummer is the heart of the band. When Carb's keepin' time, I'm feelin' fine," said Splinter.

"What are we going to do, Chip?" Gem asked.

"I don't know," Chip said. "Carb's digging bowling so much right now, he doesn't care about anything else. He thinks he's the best thing that ever hit that alley!"

"But we've got a concert this weekend," Gem said. "I don't want to mess up when we're trying to do our best to praise God!"

There are really just three main types of rocks: igneous, sedimentary, & metamorphic.

"Rocks, we've gotta get to that bowling alley," said Splinter. "Maybe we can talk some sense into him."

When they arrived at the bowling alley, they could hear rocks shouting Carb's name. "He's about to break a Rocky Ridge Bowling Rock record!" a young rock at the door told them. The place was packed with rock bowling fans. Chip, Splinter, and Gem could barely wedge in.

Suddenly everyone in the bowling alley moaned in unison. "Gutter rock!"

Carb moped over to the bench and sat with his head in his hands. He looked pretty gloomy. "Cheer up, Carb," said Gem. "Bowling isn't the most important thing in the world."

"It is to me," Carb said. "And other rocks pay attention to me when I bowl. Did you hear them shouting my name?"

"Carb, I'm sorry you didn't set any records today," said Chip. "But I think you've got it all wrong."

"That's right," said Splinter. "Bowling is *not* the most important thing in the world."

"God is!" said Gem.

Carb still looked sad. "I felt so good when all the rocks were cheering for me," he said.

"Carb," Chip said encouragingly, "rocks were made to praise God, not each other."

Carb was quiet for a minute. He thought about how much he loved to play the drums, and how great it feels to tell God how awesome he is. "Do we still have time to rehearse before dinner?" Carb asked.

"No doubt about it," said Splinter. "When Carb's keepin' time, I'm feelin' fine!"

Thinkin' It Through!

* What would you have said to Carb if you were Chip?

* Is there anything in your life more important to you than God? What is it?

* What is your favorite way to praise God?

TC TWINS TALK TEN
★ **COMMANDMENT 1:** No other gods!

When God gave his people the Ten Commandments, they had just come from Egypt where people worshiped many gods. They worshiped the sun, and their king, and even cats! God wanted his people then—and now—to know the truth. Our God is the only God, and we should not worship any other gods. God knew that it's easy to feel pressured into believing the same things as the people around you. So he reminded us that even if other people don't believe in him, we still can!

Today few of us know anyone who worships cats or the sun, but we do live in a world where it is very easy to put other things in God's place. Any time something else becomes more important to you than God—sports, school, music, your friends, or even you—you're making that thing a "god" to worship.

God wants to be number one in our lives. That means, if we have to choose between him and something else, that we choose him! Really, all of God's commandments come down to that. Jesus said that the greatest commandment is, "Love the Lord your God with all your heart and with all your soul and with all your mind" (Matthew 22:37). If we love God with all our hearts, we will want to obey him and please him. All the things he asks us to do are easy if we put him first in our lives and hearts. Maybe that's why he gave us this commandment first!

SET IN STONE: TC Twins Memory Verse

Let everything that has breath praise the Lord.

Psalm 150:6

GET ROCKIN'
WANT TO MAKE GOD #1? HERE'S HOW!

✸ When you get up each morning, listen to your favorite praise song. If the first thing you do is think about God, your day will start out the way it should.

✸ Make a list of the things that are most important to you. Thank God for those things each day.

✸ When you or your friends get really excited about a singer, or an athlete, or a movie star, remember that it's OK to admire other people, but God should still be number one!

CHAPTER 2

THE GREAT BASS DEBATE

You shall not make for yourself an idol. Exodus 20:4

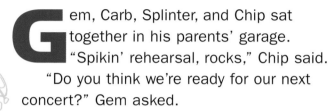

Gem, Carb, Splinter, and Chip sat together in his parents' garage. "Spikin' rehearsal, rocks," Chip said.

"Do you think we're ready for our next concert?" Gem asked.

"We're rock solid," said Chip. "That new bass guitar of Splinter's is totally sparkin'."

Gem looked at Splinter's guitar. "It's really pretty, too. I love how shiny it is."

"A guitar isn't supposed to be pretty," Splinter said. But Gem could tell he was glad she liked it.

"OK. Remember to practice at home. This concert is a boulder big deal. See you rocks on Saturday," Chip said. And everyone left—everyone except Splinter. He stayed there a long time, groovin' on his new bass.

On Saturday the band got together right before the concert to go over a few things. "OK, rocks," said Chip. "Let's do a check. Keyboards?"

"Check," said Gem, producing a cascade of notes as her fingers glided over the keys.

"Drums?"

"Check," said Carb, laying down a swell fill.

"Guitar?" said Chip. "That's me." And he let loose a lick that sent his strings to screamin'. "Check. Bass?" He waited. "Bass? Splinter, when I say bass you're supposed to say check."

"I can't say check if I don't have the bass with me," Splinter said.

"Where is it?" asked Chip.

"At home, in its case," Splinter replied.

"IN ITS CASE?!!" shouted Chip, Gem, and Carb.

"Yeah, its display case with the gold trim and the Stalactite 3000 security system," said Splinter.

"Splinter," said Chip, "I don't know how to tell you this, but your bass doesn't do us much good in its case!"

"Good rhyme, Chip. Bass and case. That's funny!" said Carb.

"Carb," said Gem, "that is *so* not the point. The point is, why is Splinter's bass guitar in some fancy display case and not here at the concert?"

The three of them stared at Splinter. How could they have a concert without him? And how could he play without his bass?

"After what you rocks said about how great my guitar was, I decided that I thought it was great, too," Splinter said.

"Yeah? So?" asked Chip. It was always hard to get a story out of Splinter.

"If my guitar is so great, then shouldn't I treat it with honor and respect?" Splinter asked. "And I sure wouldn't want anything to happen to it."

Gem said, "Splinter, the bass is great because when you *play* it, it sounds terrific."

"Yeah," said Splinter. "That baby can soar!"

"Splinter, it can't do much of anything locked up in a case," said Chip. "And it sure would be great if we had it here at our concert."

"Rocks, that bass is way too stone cold to be at this gig," said Splinter.

"But Splinter, this isn't just a gig," said Gem. "We're here to play and sing our praises to God. It sounds like you'd rather praise your silly guitar!"

"Yeah, but . . ." Splinter's voice trailed off. He thought for a minute. "You're right, rocks. I guess I was making too big of a thing out of my groovy bass." Splinter ran to get his guitar.

Chip told the stage crew to hold the show a few minutes while they finished setting up. Even though the concert started a little late, it was still the best God Rocks! concert ever. "Splinter's bass took your sound to a whole new level," said their teacher, Mrs. Crag.

"Mrs. Crag, the bass guitar won't take us very far. It's singing God's praises that will really take us places," said Splinter.

Carb *really* dug that rhyme!

! Thinkin' It Through!

* What would you have said to Splinter?

* Why do you think God told us not to worship idols?

* Are there any "idols"—things like Splinter's bass guitar— in your life? If there are, talk to God about them.

TC TWINS TALK TEN
★ COMMANDMENT 2: Don't worship idols!

What is an idol, anyway? Let's put it this way. Do you ever wish you could *see* God? Lots of people feel that way. They want to worship gods they can see and touch. So they make statues or figures out of gold or silver or wood. In fact, while Moses was up on the mountain getting the Ten Commandments from God, the people in the valley got tired of waiting for a God they couldn't see, so they made a statue of a calf and danced and sang around it. How could you believe that something you made yourself is actually a god, or magical in some way? Sounds crazy, right? That's what God says, too. He tells us in the first chapter of Romans that people with "foolish hearts" worship created things instead of the God who created them.

God has given us many wonderful gifts to enjoy, but he wants the thanks and praise to go to him, not to the gift itself. If your parents gave you a really great birthday gift, you wouldn't go up and thank the gift, would you? No! You'd thank your parents. It's the same thing with God.

Some foolish people even "worship" their sports trophies or their comic book collections or their clothes. There's nothing wrong with any of these things—the sin is in our attitude toward them. Just as with the first commandment, God is talking to us about having right priorities. We need to thank God for his good gifts, not worship them.

SET IN STONE: TC Twins Memory Verse

Do not store up for yourselves treasures on earth, where moth and rust destroy, and where thieves break in and steal.

Matthew 6:19

GET ROCKIN'
TAKE THE IDOL THING SERIOUSLY!

★ Ask your parents to help you find out about some religions that worship idols. Pray together for the people involved in those religions.

★ What makes God different from idols? Think about it, and maybe ask your parents or your Sunday school teacher what they think.

★ Even though you can't see God, you can definitely see evidence of God. The next time you wish you could just "see" God, write down all the evidence you see of God around you.

CHAPTER 3

TALKING GRAVEL

You shall not misuse the name of the Lord your God. Exodus 20:7

"Your mom makes the best lunches, Chip," Gem said, eyeing his sandwich. Her lunch sack was filled with leftovers—again. She loved her dad, Deacon Dug, but he wasn't much of a cook.

"I wish Mom would let me buy my lunch here in the cafeteria," Chip replied. "I could eat rockaroni and cheese every day of the week!" He pushed his chair out and accidentally bumped into Gran, the biggest, meanest rock in school.

Gran said something ugly to Chip. He used words that Chip's mom and dad had told him *never* to say.

"Uh, Gran, I'm sorry. I didn't see you," Chip said. "I mean, I don't know how I could miss you, with you being so big and all. Anyway, um, can I take your tray?"

"Livingstone," said Gran, "if you take my tray, I'll let it slide—this time." Then he picked up his books and headed to class.

After he left, Gem said, "Chip, did you hear what he said?"

"Yeah," said Chip. "Isn't it great? He's gonna let it slide. I'll live to see another day!"

"No, I mean before that. The words he used were disgusting," Gem said.

"What's the big deal?" said Carb. "Rocks like him talk gravel all the time."

"It's a big deal to me," said Gem. "And if you don't understand that, Carb, then I think I'll just eat my lunch somewhere else!"

Chip blows the biggest bubbles in school!

"Whoa! What did I do?" asked Carb, shrugging.

"I'm not sure, but we don't have time to find out now," replied Chip. "We'll be late for class. I'd better take the long way so I don't have to pass by Gran's locker."

Chip was glad he didn't see Gran again all afternoon. But he was worried about Gem. Why was she so upset?

After school, Chip looked for Gem, but didn't find her anywhere. *Just like Gem,* he thought. *She gets upset and takes off.* But somehow Chip had a feeling Gem might have something to be upset about. He went over to her house.

Gem was sitting on the front porch. "I've been waiting to see if you'd come by," she said.

"What's wrong, Gem?" Chip asked. "Why are you so upset about my run-in with Gran?"

"Run-in?" asked Gem. "It was more like a run-away."

"C'mon, Gem," said Chip. "That's not fair. What's going on?"

"Did you hear the way Gran used God's name?" Gem asked.

"It would have been hard *not* to hear it," replied Chip.

"But you didn't say anything to him about it," Gem said.

"Gem, if you'll recall, Gran is about two tons heavier than me. He's not a rock I like to challenge."

"Don't you remember what we saw at the God Rocks Hall of Fame last week? The smooth stone told us about how David slung a rock at Goliath."

"Did you want me to sling my lunch at Gran?" Chip asked.

"No. But if David was brave enough to stand up to Goliath when Goliath insulted God, I think you should have been brave enough to tell Gran not to use God's name that way," Gem said.

Chip thought for a minute and winked as he said, "You know, Gem, you're really annoying when you're right."

"I do my best," Gem said with a smile.

The next day, Chip *didn't* avoid the hallway where Gran's locker was. Gran saw him coming. "Livingstone," he said, "are you looking for trouble?"

"I'm not, Gran, but you might be," Chip said. Gran was obviously caught off guard. Chip went on to tell Gran how important God's name is, and that God has said to use it respectfully.

"Rock," Gran said, "I didn't mean nothin' by it. That's just how I talk."

Chip said, "How would you like it if I used your name as a nasty word? What if I said 'Oh, Gran!' to myself whenever anything bad happened?"

This time *Gran* cracked a smile. "I see your point, Livingstone. Just don't bowl me over in the cafeteria next time, OK?"

Gran and Chip weren't exactly best friends after that, but Chip never worried about passing Gran's locker again!

Thinkin' It Through!

* Do you think Gem got too upset about what Gran said? What would you have done?

* Do you ever say things that would make Gem mad if she heard them?

* What do you think about how Chip handled the situation?

TC TWINS TALK TEN
★ **COMMANDMENT 3:** Don't misuse God's name!

Do you know the story behind your name? Maybe you were named after a movie star your mom likes, or your dad's best friend. Maybe your name was chosen because of its special meaning, or because it reflects your ethnic background. However you got it, your name is important to you. For you, it's more than just a group of letters; it represents who you are.

God's name is very important, too. It's so special that for a long time people didn't even know what it was! When God appeared to Moses to tell him to go back to Egypt and free the Hebrew slaves, Moses asked God to tell his name. God said his name is "I AM." That name is so special that for many years the Hebrew people wouldn't say it out loud, and if they had to write it, they took a bath first! Then they threw away the pen they used,

Rockin' with the Rules!

because a pen that wrote God's name was too good to be used to write any other word ever again.

God meant for us to treat his name with special respect. That's why he tells us not to misuse it in the third commandment. If his name is so holy that some people won't even say it, it's pretty obvious that it's not OK to yell it out when you stub your toe or see something really cool. That's what "in vain" means.

God *definitely* wants you to talk to him. And it's fine to use his name when you do. But don't use it as a swear word. That's not a way to respect God!

SET IN STONE: TC Twins Memory Verse

Our Father in heaven, hallowed be your name.

Matthew 6:9

GET ROCKIN'
HERE'S HOW YOU CAN HONOR GOD'S NAME!

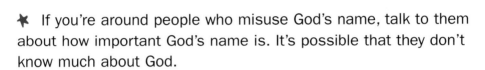

★ If you're around people who misuse God's name, talk to them about how important God's name is. It's possible that they don't know much about God.

★ Ask your parents or a friend to let you know if they hear you misusing God's name. Sometimes we say things without thinking, and it helps to know someone else is listening.

★ Don't just avoid misusing God's name, use it the *right* way. Talk to him right now! Tell him what's going on in your life.

CHAPTER 4

GIVE IT A REST!

Remember the Sabbath day by keeping it holy. Exodus 20:8

"**C**hip! Nuggie!" Cliff shouted. "Hurry up or we'll be late for church."

Chip rushed into the kitchen with his dog, Ruff, at his heels. "Mom, did you make the Rock Crispie Treats? I've got to take a snack to Sunday school."

"Sure did, Chip. I got up early this morning and made them. I hope I can stay awake during Pastor Jasper's sermon."

"Sugar rock, did you remember the casserole for the pot rock lunch?" Cliff asked Ruby as he grabbed his Bible.

"No. We'll stop by the store after church. We need to hurry. Where's Nuggie?"

"I'm coming!" Nuggie said. "I just want to finish looking over my memory verse."

"We don't have time for that!" said Chip. "We've got to go!"

Nuggie watched as her family ran to the car. Her mom was carrying an enormous plate of Rock Crispie Treats. Chip turned around to go back to the house for something he forgot. CRASH!

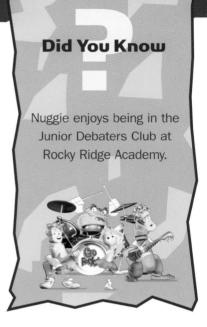
Crispie Treats went everywhere. "No time to stop," said Cliff. "Let's go!"

When they got in the car, Chip turned on the radio. "Mom," he said, "Don't forget my game at 2:00 this afternoon."

"And I've got a Cornerstones meeting at 3:30," said Cliff.

"We're supposed to have dinner at Splinter's house tonight," reminded Chip.

"I've got to weed before the judging of 'Rock Garden of the Year' tomorrow," Ruby said.

"And I've got band practice tonight!" groaned Chip.

"I don't know how we will get it all done," said Cliff. "Here's the church. Let's go! Hurry!"

Cliff, Ruby, and Chip jumped out of the car and rushed off. Nuggie picked up her Bible and slowly unbuckled her seatbelt. "Why all the hurry?" she said to herself as she walked in to church.

The entry of Stone Church was packed with people rushing this way and that. Good friends stopped only a moment to say hello as they hurried off. Nuggie noticed a family of rocks she had never seen before. They looked a little lost, but everyone just rushed right past them.

Did You Know

Sedimentary rocks are made when layers of "sediment" (a fancy name for stuff like gravel) get smushed together.

As usual, Cliff, Ruby, Chip, and Nuggie sat together to listen to Pastor Jasper's sermon. Nuggie watched as Chip scribbled notes during the sermon.

Afterward, Nuggie said, "Chip, I've never seen you take so many notes during the sermon before!"

Chip said, "Who has time for notes? I was writing a schedule of everything I have to do this afternoon!"

"Really, son?" Cliff said. "Let's see."

"No time for that now," Ruby said, trying to shuffle everyone out the door. "We have to run!"

"HOLD IT, EVERYBODY!" shouted Nuggie. "What are you all doing?"

"Haven't you been listening, dear?" said Ruby. "Chip has a game, your father has a meeting, but first there's lunch, and then—"

"But mom," interrupted Nuggie. "I thought Sundays were supposed to be special!"

"Sundays are special, dear," said Cliff. "Especially busy."

"No, I mean special for God!" Nuggie said. "Do you think God wants us to be so busy that Chip writes out his schedule during the sermon?"

"Nuggie may be on to something," said Chip. "We talked in Sunday school today about how God wanted us to keep one day a week holy."

"What does 'holy' mean, Chip?" Nuggie asked.

"Like you said. Set apart. Special. God took six days to make the world, which means he was way busier those days than we are. But on the seventh day, he rested."

"You mean instead of running around like crazy, we're supposed to be *resting*?" Nuggie asked.

"Yes, Nuggie," said Ruby. "You're right. We have let our Sundays get a little bit out of control."

"A *little* bit?" said Nuggie. "Dad wore his gym shoes to church so he could run faster down the aisle!"

"Never again," Cliff said. "From now on, Sundays are going to be a time for us to be together, think about God—"

"And rest!" said Ruby, Chip, and Nuggie in unison.

Thinkin' It Through!

* Does your family ever seem rushed on Sundays? How does that make you feel?

* What do you do on Sunday (such as go to church) that makes it a special day?

* What might Chip, Cliff, and Ruby miss out on if they stay busy all day on Sunday?

TC TWINS TALK TEN
★ **COMMANDMENT 4:** Remember the Sabbath!

Sometimes it seems like there just isn't enough time in the day. You may have soccer games, or dance class, or piano lessons, or hockey. Then there's homework. Ugh! And chores around the house. Of course you want to spend time with your friends, too. And you've got to eat!

God knows us really well, though. He knows that we need to rest and take time to think about him, too. Maybe that's why he commanded the Israelites to set aside the Sabbath as a holy day of rest. He didn't just stop there, either. God said that the animals they used to work the land needed a day of rest, too (Exodus 23:12). And even the land needed to rest. After planting crops on a piece of land for six years in a row, the Israelites were supposed to let the land rest for a whole year (Exodus 23:10).

So what does it mean to keep the Sabbath as a holy day of rest? The Israelites worshipped God on Saturday, the Sabbath. But after that rock rolled away from Jesus' tomb on a Sunday, Christians have worshipped God on Sunday instead. So we can apply God's Sabbath ideas to our Sundays. You can keep Sunday holy by spending time learning about God in church. You can hang out with your family. And you can spend special time on Sundays talking to God.

It's up to you and your family to figure out how to keep your day of rest "holy." But remember that God loves you and he's got some pretty good ideas about how your life will work best!

SET IN STONE: TC Twins Memory Verse

Jesus said, "Come to me, all you who are weary and burdened, and I will give you rest."

Matthew 11:28

GET ROCKIN'
HERE ARE SOME RESTFUL WAYS TO KEEP YOUR SABBATH HOLY!

✱ Get everything ready for church ahead of time. Figure out what you're going to wear, remind your parents of anything you're supposed to take to church, and go to bed on time. This may not sound like fun, but it will help.

✱ Plan some just-you-and-God time on Sundays. Read a Bible story and ask God what he wants you to take away from it.

✱ Remember that Sunday isn't the only day to think about God. God really wants to be a part of your life every day of the week! Spend time every day reading your Bible and talking to him.

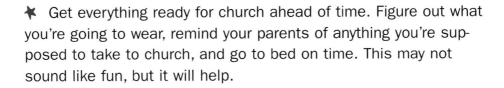

CHAPTER 5

A SOGGY SURPRISE

Honor your father and your mother, so that you may live long in the land the Lord your God is giving you. Exodus 20:12

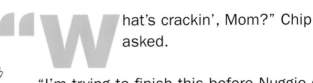

"**W**hat's crackin', Mom?" Chip asked.

"I'm trying to finish this before Nuggie gets home from school," his mom answered. "Would you like to help?"

"Sure!" Chip said. "What can I do?"

"Your father and I are planning a surprise birthday party for your little sister. You can help me finish these invitations to her friends."

"A surprise party—for Nuggie? She's just a kid!" Chip grumbled.

"What was that, dear?"

"Nothing," Chip mumbled. "I'd help, but I think I'd better get busy with my homework."

"That's OK. I'll just finish these up," Ruby said.

Chip trudged up to his room. His dog, Ruff, ran to greet him. Chip muttered, "Maybe someday you'll throw me a surprise party—nobody else ever has." Chip flipped on his rock blaster. Nothing happened. "What's going on?" He looked at it. Covered in seaweed! "Aw, rocks! Nuggie must have been trying to get her fish to dance again. She dropped my blaster in the aquarium!" Chip loved his little sister, most of the time, but he *hated* when she messed with his stuff. He ran to tell his mom.

CRASH! Chip slammed into his dad, Cliff, in the hallway.

"Whoa, slow down there, son," his dad said. "This isn't an avalanche zone! What's the rush?"

"Dad, Nuggie's been in my stuff again, and this time she ruined my blaster. Now I can't listen to my favorite tunes!"

"Hmm? I'm sure it was an accident, Chip. We'll talk about it later. Right now, I've got to hide Nuggie's new bike before she sees it!"

She gets a new bike, thought Chip, *and all I have is a soggy rock blaster. Nuggie doesn't deserve all this good stuff. What are Mom and Dad thinking?*

"CHIP!" his mom called. "When you're done with you're homework, come down and help me make a Happy Birthday banner for Nuggie!"

"I gotta get out of here!" Chip groaned. He slid out the back door and headed toward Gem's house. Along the way he ran into Carb.

"Hey, man, what's grinding you?" Carb asked.

"My parents. They're throwing a surprise party for Nuggie AND getting her a new bike, even though she soaked my rock blaster!"

"I don't get parents," Carb said.

When they got to Gem's house, Splinter was there, too. "Did you bring your blaster, Chip?" Gem asked. "I want to play Concrete's new song, 'God Is Stalag-mighty'!"

"His little sister soaked it," Carb said.

"That's rough. That's mighty rough," said Splinter.

"And his parents are throwing her a surprise birthday party!" added Carb.

"Don't remind me," said Chip. "Nuggie is SO spoiled! Sometimes my parents really get me down."

"That's too bad about your rock blaster, Chip," said Gem. "But aren't you forgetting the party your parents gave us after our first big concert? That was pretty cool!"

"Yeah, they invited half the town to celebrate," said Carb.

"I think you're just upset because your blaster got soaked," Splinter added.

"Don't be too hard on your parents, Chip. Remember what the Ten Commandment Twins told us."

"Yeah, be sure to turn out the lights when you leave the exhibit."

"No, Chip," said Gem. "'Honor your father and mother.'"

"So?" asked Chip.

"Complaining about your parents to your friends isn't exactly honoring them. Why don't you tell them how you're feeling?"

"Yeah, maybe." said Chip. "See you rocks later."

When Chip got home, his mom and dad were waiting for him. "We were getting a little worried," said his mom.

"And Nuggie feels awful about your rock blaster," his dad chimed in. "I'll loan you ours until yours gets fixed."

"Thanks, Dad. I guess I was mad that you were throwing Nuggie a party she doesn't deserve."

"Parents give their kids all kinds of things they don't deserve," his dad said. "We give you gifts because we love you, not because you've earned them."

"That shouldn't come as a surprise to a smart stone, like you," said his mom.

"I guess you're right," Chip said. "I'm sorry for being so upset. Can I help put out the party hats?"

! Thinkin' It Through!

* Have you ever been mad at your parents before? What did you do?

* Parents often give their children gifts they don't "deserve." How is that like what God does for his children?

* What do you think about how Chip reacted to his parents? What might you have done differently?

TC TWINS TALK TEN

★ **COMMANDMENT 5:** Honor your father and mother.

Compared with murder and stealing, dishonoring your parents doesn't really seem like a big deal, does it? Have you ever wondered why God made this one of his "top ten" rules to live by?

Paul says in Romans 13:1, "Everyone must submit himself to the governing authorities, for there is no authority except that which God has established." If God wants us to submit to the authority of the people who run our school and our country, how much more does he want us to submit to our parents?

As with everything else God has done, this policy makes a lot of sense. Your parents aren't perfect (nobody's are), but they love you and want what's best for you. When you were little, you may not have understood why your mom wouldn't let you touch a hot stove, or why your dad wouldn't let you cross the street by yourself. But aren't you glad they were there to protect you? Believe it or not, there are dangers and problems in this world that your parents still know more about than you do. When they suggest that a certain person might not make a good friend, they know what they are talking about.

Does that mean everything your parents say is right? Maybe not. No one knows everything except God. But even when your parents make mistakes, you can still honor them. They've done a lot for you, and they deserve your respect. Also, God knows that if you are willing to obey and honor your parents, it will be easier for you to obey and honor him.

SET IN STONE: TC Twins Memory Verse

Children, obey your parents in everything, for this pleases the Lord.

Colossians 3:20

GET ROCKIN'
HERE ARE SOME SPARKIN' WAYS TO HONOR YOUR PARENTS!

✱ Give your parents "coupons" for shoulder rubs, breakfast in bed, or extra chores (not chores that you're already supposed to be doing).

✱ Ask your grandparents to tell you stories about when your parents were your age. Sometimes it's easier to see your parents as "real people" when you hear about them from someone else.

✱ Pray for your parents. Hey, raising you isn't easy!

Rockin' with the Rules!

CHAPTER 6

GAMES ROCKS PLAY

You shall not murder. Exodus 20:13

"**D**id you see that?" Carb asked Splinter as they walked out of the Rocky Ridge movie theater. "He crushed that rock to powder!"

"Very low-down," said Splinter. "Sparkin'."

"That movie was even better the fourth time. I caught so many more cool fight moves than I had before," Carb said.

"Let's go back to your place, rock," said Splinter.

"Yeah! I've rented the new Death Rock 3000 video game—unless you're too scared to play." Splinter was up to the challenge.

Death Rock 3000 was a terrific game. The players chased after other rocks and pushed them off cliffs or into volcanoes. The sparkin' graphics let them watch every detail of the rocks being smashed into a million pieces! The player who smashed the most rocks got to be Death Rock Champion.

"Looks like no other rock can beat me," boasted Splinter. "Rocks of the world, beware!"

"Don't worry, Splinter," Carb said. "Next time I'll crush you!"

They went to find Chip to tell him about the new things they saw in the movie. Splinter also wanted to brag about being Death Rock 3000 Champ again!

When they got to Chip's, his mom, Ruby, answered the door. "Hello you two," she said. "Come on in. Chip is in his room. We're expecting a visit from Pastor Jasper at any minute, but you are welcome to stay."

"Thank you, Mrs. Livingstone," they said, and headed for Chip's room.

Chip was lying on his bed next to his dog, Ruff. Ruff jumped up to greet Splinter and Carb. "How was the movie *this* time?" Chip asked.

"It was cool!"

"Let's go grab a snack and you can tell me all about it," Chip said.

Carb didn't waste a minute. "Remember how The Abolisher always made the crooked rocks jump into the volcano? We noticed this time that the lava was so hot, a couple of them melted before they landed!"

Then Splinter jumped in, "And I'm the new Death Rock 3000 Champion!"

"Death Rock 3000?" asked a voice behind them. It was Pastor Jasper. He was the minister at Stone Church. The boys all really liked the great stories he told. Sometimes they thought he must be God's best friend.

"Yeah!" said Splinter. "It's the most sparkin' game I've ever played."

Pastor Jasper turned and asked, "What makes it so, um, sparkin', do you think?"

"You get to push rocks off cliffs and watch them get smashed to bits!" Carb said.

Pastor Jasper thought for a minute. "I'm not sure about this game. What's so fun about crushing other rocks?" he asked.

The boys didn't know how to answer. They thought that Pastor Jasper must see something wrong with the game, but they weren't sure what.

"I hate to spoil your fun, boys," said the pastor. "I'm just not sure it's a good idea for you to play games like 'Death Rock 3000.' Or see violent movies again and again."

"Four times, actually," said Carb.

"I know those movies and games seem really cool, but God doesn't want us filling our eyes and heads with things that are destructive, just for the fun of it," said Pastor Jasper. "In real life, blasting other rocks is a terrible thing."

"But those rocks don't really die," said Carb. "It's just a show."

"But God's creation should never be blasted just for fun—even when pretending," said Pastor Jasper.

Splinter saw his point. Chip thought about how glad Gem would be if they stopped going to those movies. But Carb asked, "Well then, what are we supposed to do?"

Pastor Jasper looked around the kitchen. "I bet Mrs. Livingstone has a rockleberry pie somewhere around here. I don't know about you, but I'd rather eat pie than go see those movies any day!"

Thinkin' It Through!

* Do the TV shows you watch show people hurting each other?

* What do you think about what Pastor Jasper said? Do you think violence in TV, movies, and games is a big deal?

* Why do you think so many TV shows and movies show violence? What can you do to help change the amount of violence around you?

TC TWINS TALK TEN
★ **COMMANDMENT 6:** Do not murder!

Do you think it's cool to watch movies with lots of guns and blood? If you do, you're not alone. Movie companies keep making movies like that because people keep buying tickets to go see them. Sometimes they are interesting and the special effects can be great. It's fun to see the good guys win and the bad guys get what's coming to them. But are those really the kinds of things God wants us to see?

The sixth commandment tells us not to murder. But God had told people how important human life was long before that. When the very first brothers, Cain and Abel, both offered gifts to God, Cain got mad because God liked Abel's gift better. Cain got so mad that he murdered Abel! God knew that we would sometimes get so mad that we might hurt and even kill other people.

You may think you can obey this commandment with no problem. After all, even if you yell at your little sister and say, "I'm gonna kill you," you don't really mean it, right? Jesus said something interesting about that. He said that if you hate another person, you have broken this commandment in your heart.

So be careful about what you watch. Don't fill your mind with lots of violence. And be careful what you say, too. Words can hurt almost as much as knives and guns!

SET IN STONE: TC Twins Memory Verse

Choose life . . . that you may love the Lord your God, listen to his voice, and hold fast to him.

Deuteronomy 30:19, 20

GET ROCKIN'
TOO MUCH VIOLENCE?
MAKE SOME CHANGES!

✸ If you get angry with someone, talk to God *and* to that person. It's better to be honest (in a kind way) about how you feel than to let angry feelings build up until you want to hurt someone.

✸ Be careful about the kinds of movies, TV, and video games you see. Having lots of violent pictures in your head can make violence seem like no big deal.

✸ Before going to a movie, find out how much violence it has. Consider staying away. Have a list of fun things you can choose to do instead when you need to make that hard decision.

CHAPTER 7

LOVE ROCKS

You shall not commit adultery. Exodus 20:14

"**M**om!" said Nuggie. "You look great!" Nuggie and Chip's mom, Ruby, looked at herself in the mirror. She was wearing her favorite flower necklace, and she had on the new fancy perfume she had gotten in Rocktropolis.

"Do you think your dad will like the new perfume?" she asked.

"It's great, Mom," said Chip. "And Dad will love the special dinner you made for him."

Today was the Livingstones' wedding anniversary. Ruby knew that her husband, Cliff, had been having a hard time. His job as an editor for the *Rocky Ridge TIMES* had been a little rocky lately. She wanted to treat him to a special evening. Nuggie and Chip had eaten earlier and promised to stay in their rooms to give their parents some time alone. And since it was a special occasion, Chip even agreed to do his homework without being reminded.

"Everything is ready! I hope your father gets home before dinner gets cold!" Ruby said.

Cliff's beverage of choice is iced rockuccinos from the café in town.

Ten minutes went by. Then twenty more. Then an hour. And Cliff still wasn't home. Finally, the phone rang. Chip answered. "Hi, Son!" Cliff said over the phone. "Tell your mom I'll be home late tonight. I've got to rewrite the lead story and get it on the press for the early morning edition."

"Dad," Chip said. "I think you'd better come home. Mom—"

"Oh, Son," Cliff interrupted. "I'm sure your mother will understand," and he hung up the phone.

No, Dad, Chip thought to himself. *I'm pretty sure she won't.*

Chip dreaded having to tell the news to his mom, so he gave her a hug and broke it to her as gently as he could. But the news still made her cry a little. Chip felt awful.

"Would you like to play one of my video games with me?" he asked.

"That's very sweet of you, Chip," his mom said between sniffles. "But why don't you and Nuggie go on to bed? I'm just going to lie here on the couch and wait for your father. I'm sure he'll be home soon."

Did You Know

Caves are formed out of rock by water. The process forms stalag*tites* that cling tightly to the ceiling, and stalag*mites* that might reach the top!

Chip was sad, and even a little worried. But he did what his mom asked him to do and told Nuggie to get ready for bed, too. As Chip put on his pajamas, he began to wonder about the rocks he knew at school. Some of their parents didn't live in the same house anymore because they fought so much. *That would never happen to my parents,* Chip thought, *or would it?*

Just then, Ruff came trotting into his room. *Hey, boy, how's Mom?* Chip asked. Ruff barked and wagged his tail excitedly. *You're right, Ruff. I'd better go check on her. She was really sad.*

Chip walked into the living room. He saw *two* people sitting on the couch. His parents! And they weren't fighting. In fact, they were—kissing! And his mom was holding some beautiful flowers!

"Chip," said Ruby. "We . . . uh . . . didn't hear you come in."

"So," Chip said. "You aren't mad at each other?"

"Mad?!" said Cliff. "Of course not! We're just celebrating our anniversary! Do you like your mom's flowers?"

"Yes, but I thought you were fighting," Chip said. "And—what about dinner?"

"I was upset, dear," said Ruby. "But I've forgiven your father. He didn't know he was going to have to work late."

"And I can't wait to dig into that special dinner your mom made," said Cliff. "Even if it is cold!"

"No matter what happens," Ruby said as she smiled sweetly at Cliff, "your father and I will always love each other."

"How do you know?" Chip asked.

"Because we made a promise," Cliff said, "to God and to each other to always be true to each other."

"Chip, what are you doing in the living room?" asked Nuggie as she came around the corner rubbing her eyes. "Shouldn't you go to bed and let Mom and Dad be alone? After all, it is their anniversary!"

"Nuggie," said Chip, "you are a genius! After all, who wants to see his parents *kissing*?"

Thinkin' It Through!

* Why did Ruby forgive Cliff?

* What does it mean to keep promises?

* Why is it important to keep your promises?

TC TWINS TALK TEN
★ COMMANDMENT 7: Be faithful to your mate.

The seventh commandment tells married people to be faithful. Husbands and wives are close in ways that should be saved just for each other.

You probably know people who aren't married anymore. Maybe even your parents are divorced. If they are, you know better than anyone how hard it can be, and why God told us how important it is for husbands and wives to be loyal and faithful.

Remember that if parents get divorced, it is not the kid's fault! Just as you and only you are responsible for what you do, your parents, NOT YOU, are responsible for what they do.

Also remember that God loves us and wants to forgive us and heal us from the pain of sin. If your parents have problems, go to God for comfort. If you have friends whose parents have problems, try to be understanding and encouraging.

Rockin' with the Rules!

One thing God tells us is that we should not be "yoked" with unbelievers (2 Corinthians 6). What does that mean? One thing it means is that God doesn't want us to marry people who do not also believe in him. A yoke connects two oxen together so they can pull a plow. When you're yoked with someone, you have to go the same direction he or she does. So it's a good idea to "yoke" yourself to someone who wants to follow God's direction.

Remember, everybody has some problems, and just because parents fight doesn't mean they will split up. Lots of people have very happy marriages—and that really pleases God!

SET IN STONE: TC Twins Memory Verse

Above all, love each other deeply, because love covers over a multitude of sins.

1 Peter 4:8

GET ROCKIN'
HOW CAN YOU BE TRUE AFTER
YOU SAY, "I DO"? HERE ARE SOME TIPS!

✖ Being faithful to your mate means being the kind of person who keeps promises. So start practicing now! Do what you say you will do when you say you will do it.

✖ Be careful about the kinds of TV shows and movies you watch. Lots of shows make it look sparkin' to behave in ways that don't respect God's plan for marriage.

✖ Ask your parents or other married adults you know to tell you the story of how they met and fell in love.

CHAPTER 8

PICK UP STICKS

You shall not steal. Exodus 20:15

"OK, Carb, I dare you to crash your cymbals in class," Splinter said.

"Yeah, that would really scare the gravel out of Mrs. Crag!" Chip said.

Carb never said no to a dare. He grabbed some cymbals, tip-toed back to his desk, raised his hands, and—"

"Carb, don't you do it!" Mrs. Crag said. *Busted!* thought Carb.

"That's OK, rock," said Splinter. "You will just have to make up the dare this afternoon—at the Fossil Fair Mall." Fossil Fair Mall was the best place in town to hang out, and it had a sparkin' music store, the Whack Shack.

"Great," said Carb. "I can pick up some new drumsticks. I tore mine up on rim shots at our last concert."

That afternoon, Carb, Splinter, and Chip headed for the mall. As soon as they got there, Carb dared Chip to jump in the fountain. Chip did it, but the fountain was a lot deeper than it looked, so he came out looking like Ruff does after his bath. Next Chip dared Splinter to turn cartwheels through the food court, shouting, "Rocks rule! Plants drool!" He made quite a mess when he crashed into the rock candy cart. The friends quickly helped clean up.

Then Carb said, "Hey, I want to get to the Whack Shack before it closes."

The Whack Shack had *everything*— guitars, keyboards, drum sets, posters of all their favorite rock bands, and every- thing else a rock musician could want. Carb headed straight for the drum sec- tion. "Whoa, these sticks are more expensive than I thought," he said.

"Carb," Splinter said, "it's your turn to take a dare."

"You name it," Carb said. "I'll do it."

"Here it is," said Splinter. But as he bent over to whisper his dare to Carb, a rock from school came around the end of the aisle.

"I dare you to take those drumsticks out of the store without paying for them." It was Gran! He was the school bully who was always giving these rocks a hard time.

"You mean swipe them?" asked Carb.

"Shhh. Not so loud." Gran answered. "Just walk out with them. The store will never miss one set."

Carb thought for a minute. Carb hated to turn down a dare. "I double-rock dare you," said Gran.

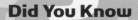

"A double-rock dare?" echoed Carb as he looked at Splinter for help. No rock had ever turned down a double-rock dare!

"Carb, I don't know," said Splinter.

Chip came over. "What's going on, rocks?" he asked. When he saw Gran, he knew it couldn't be good.

"Carb is going to back out on a double-rock dare," said Splinter.

"No way!" Chip said.

"Your friend is too scared," said Gran.

Carb quickly reached for the drumsticks and started to put them in his pocket.

"What are you doing?" Chip asked.

"Gran's dare. He dared me to swipe the drumsticks," Carb replied.

"It's no big deal. It's not like stealing a car," said Gran.

Splinter's knees were shaking but he managed to blurt out, "Don't do it, man! What if you get caught?"

"He won't get caught if he does it right," said Gran.

"It's not just that," said Chip, looking worried. "My dad always said that it's wrong to take things that don't belong to you."

Carb just stood there holding the drumsticks. Then he put them back on the shelf. "I may be the first rock in the history of Rocky Ridge to turn down a double-rock dare, but I just can't take those sticks."

Gran shrugged and said, "You rocks are soft!" Then, to everyone's relief, he just walked away.

"Whew! That was a close one," said Splinter. "What made you change your mind?"

"Like Chip said, I don't want to take something that belongs to someone else," replied Carb. "I wouldn't like it if someone took something that belonged to me."

"Besides," said Chip, "We're The God Rocks! We can't exactly praise God if our drummer is using stolen sticks!"

"Good point. Now, where were we?" asked Splinter. "Oh, yeah, Carb still has to take a dare!"

"You name it," Carb said.

"I dare you to let me use the money I got for my birthday to buy you a new set of drumsticks."

Carb *took* that dare.

Thinkin' It Through!

★ Why do you think people steal things?

★ If Carb had stolen the drumsticks, he might not have gotten caught. Would that have made it OK?

★ What would you do if someone dared you to steal or do something else you know is wrong?

TC TWINS TALK TEN

★ **COMMANDMENT 8:** Do not steal.

God's command that we should not steal may be one of the easiest to understand. Jesus told his disciples, "Do to others what you would have them do to you" (Matthew 7:12). No one wants to have stuff stolen, so it's easy to see why God would tell us not to steal from other people.

Sometimes people steal without realizing it. Some people think it is no big deal to take little things that just seem to be "lying around." Others, like Gran, think it can't hurt too much to take something small from a big store. After all, who will miss it? Who will ever know?

God will know. And with all the security cameras stores have now, there's a good chance the store manager will know, too. If you know someone who thinks it's a good joke to take stuff from stores, you might want to give that friendship a second thought.

Why *do* people steal things, anyway? Stealing is wrong because we shouldn't take what belongs to other people, but it's also wrong because we shouldn't grab for things God hasn't provided to us. If you steal something, it's kind of like telling God that the stuff he's given you isn't good enough. You want more.

Just keep in mind that stealing anything—from a paper clip to a car—is outside of what God wants for you. He wants to give you good things! So if anyone ever "dares" you to steal—or anything else you know is wrong—remember that there is *nothing* brave about breaking God's rules.

SET IN STONE: TC Twins Memory Verse

Do to others what you would have them do to you.

Matthew 7:12

GET ROCKIN'
HERE ARE THREE WAYS TO DO
THE RIGHT THING!

✸ Don't hang out with people who think it's sparkin' to steal. The Bible says that bad company corrupts good character. That just means that even if you want to do the right thing, you probably won't, if you hang out with people who do wrong things.

✸ Return stuff you borrow! Look around your room right now to see if there is anything that belongs to someone else, and take it back.

✸ If someone does steal something from you, let an adult know. But ask God to help you forgive the person who hurt you.

CHAPTER 9

LITTLE WHITE LIES

You shall not give false testimony against
your neighbor. Exodus 20:16

"Nuggie," her dad, Cliff, said, "Did you finish your project for school tomorrow?"

"Sure did, Dad," Nuggie said. "Pretty much, anyway," she whispered.

"Great!" said Cliff. "Let's go get some ice cream!"

Ruby, Cliff, and Nuggie headed for the ice cream parlor. "Where's Chip?" Nuggie asked.

"He wasn't done with his homework, so he couldn't come," Ruby replied.

Nuggie's face turned a little red. She hadn't exactly *finished* her project, either. And the next morning, her mom and dad found out.

"Come on, Sugar Rock," Ruby said to Nuggie. "The school bus is here."

"I don't think I can go to school today," Nuggie said. "I don't feel so good."

"I knew we shouldn't let you eat ice cream so late at night!" her mom said. "You just go back to bed and don't worry about a thing. I'll give the doctor a call. It's a good thing you finished your school project last night. Your father can drop it off on his way to work."

Nuggie groaned. "You do feel terrible, don't you," her mom said.

"I do now," Nuggie replied. "Mom, I have to tell you something. I'm not really sick."

"I don't understand, dear. You do look a little pale."

"That's because I didn't exactly tell the truth last night when I said I'd finished my project. I was *almost* finished. I thought I could finish when I got home. And I *really* wanted ice cream!"

"So you were pretending to be sick so you wouldn't have to go to school?" Ruby asked.

"Uh-huh," said Nuggie.

"And, remember last week, when you told me that it was Chip, not you, who forgot to let Ruff out? Was that a lie, too?"

"Uh-huh," said Nuggie.

"Sugar Rock, I think maybe you are sick after all," Ruby said.

"What do you mean, Mom?" Nuggie asked.

"Sin is a sickness. A sickness of the heart and soul. And those lies you've been telling are sins," Ruby said.

"I didn't know it was a sin to lie!" Nuggie said.

"Did telling those lies make you feel bad inside?" her mom asked.

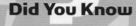

"They sure did. My tummy felt so bad this morning that it almost wasn't a lie when I said I was sick!"

"When you feel bad about something you did, that can be a sign that what you did was wrong," Ruby said.

Nuggie was very, very sorry she lied, and very, very sorry she had to go to school without her project done!

That afternoon, Ruby was waiting for Nuggie when she got off the school bus. Chip wouldn't get home from school until later that day, so Nuggie and her mom went for a walk.

"How was your day at school, Sugar Rock?" Ruby asked.

"Not so good. When Mrs. Crag asked about my project, I wanted to tell her the truth, but instead I told her that Ruff had chewed it up!" Nuggie cried.

"Did she believe you?" Ruby asked.

"No, Mom, she didn't. Last week I had told her that a bird swooped down and stole my homework out of my hands. I think she might call you and Dad."

"I was afraid of this," Ruby said. She told Nuggie that telling lies can become a habit. "When we tell one lie, we have to tell another lie to cover it up. Then it seems like all we're doing is lying."

Nuggie was beginning to understand. "That's what I do," she said. "I don't want to be a big liar all my life!"

"If you start practicing now, you'll be a big truth-teller all your life, instead," said Mom.

When they got home, Chip was there. "Nuggie!" he yelled. "Where is my spikin' new hat?"

"I think Dad took it," she said. Nuggie gasped and covered her mouth quickly with her hand. Nuggie had already forgotten what she was supposed to start practicing. "I mean, I borrowed it when I was playing dress-up. I'm sorry, Chip."

"That's OK," Chip said. "You can have it. I can get another one. Thanks for telling me the truth."

"Mom," Nuggie said. "I think I'm going to like practicing the habit of telling the truth!"

Thinkin' It Through!

* Why do you think Nuggie kept telling lies?

* Is it ever OK to lie?

* What happened when Nuggie told the truth?

TC TWINS TALK TEN
★ COMMANDMENT 9: Do not give false testimony.

The ninth commandment tells us not to give "false testimony" about a neighbor. That means more than just the person next door to you. Our neighbor is anyone around us. But what is "false testimony"? Think about a trial in a courtroom. If you were called to be a witness in a case, and you lied about what you saw or knew, that would be "false testimony." You would be hurting the person you lied about, and keeping people from knowing the truth.

We can give "false testimony" about ourselves, too. Nuggie lied about her homework so she could get ice cream. She didn't want her parents to know the truth. But in the end, all those lies made her feel really bad, and made it hard for anyone to believe her. If something ever really did happen to her homework, her teacher probably wouldn't believe her. Would you?

Rockin' with the Rules!

Nuggie also learned that telling lies can become a habit. Some people lie so much that they don't even realize it. They don't even get that sick feeling in their stomachs that Nuggie got when she lied, because they are so used to lying. It's pretty sad when you do a wrong thing so often that you don't even realize it. But just because you don't realize it doesn't mean people around you don't, either. No one wants to be friends with someone who can't be trusted.

Make a decision to give *true* testimony about all that you see and do. That way, you'll get in the truth-telling habit! It's a good habit to have.

SET IN STONE: TC Twins Memory Verse

Speaking the truth in love, we will in all things grow up into . . . Christ.

Ephesians 4:15

GET ROCKIN'
WANT TO GET INTO THE TRUTH-TELLING HABIT? HERE'S HOW!

★ If you need to tell someone the truth, but it seems too hard, write it down! That way you can think about the words you want to use, and you don't have to worry about "chickening out."

★ Talk to your family about truth-telling. Sometimes even grown ups tell "little white lies." But even "little" lies are big to God. Ask your parents to have an all-truth house!

★ Have you told a lie recently? If so, go right now (or as soon as you can) and tell the truth!

CHAPTER 10

GEM GETS GREEN

You shall not covet . . . anything that belongs to your neighbor. Exodus 20:17

"Wow, Amber," said Gem. "Those are sparkin' boots!" Amber was the new girl in school. Her parents owned a chain of Rockcastle restaurants.

"Oh, these old things?" said Amber. "I was thinking about getting rid of them. I've had them for ages." Amber shut her locker and headed to class.

Gem watched Amber walk down the hall. Amber had *every-thing. Her* clothes weren't from the sale rack! Gem *really* wanted some new boots, but her dad said that she'd have to wait awhile.

"Hey, Gem," said Chip, coming up behind her. "Are you coming to Rocky Road's after school?"

"Why?" Gem asked. "What's going on?"

"Remember, Amber's taking us all for ice cream. Isn't that terrific?"

"Yeah, terrific," Gem muttered as Chip headed to class. "If you got invited."

Gem was miserable all day at school. She forgot her books for first period and dropped a beaker in biology. Mrs. Crag even offered to send her to see the school nurse.

"No, thank you, Mrs. Crag," Gem said. "I'm not sick."

But she *felt* sick. All she could think about was Amber. And about all the things Amber had that she didn't. Gem decided that

she didn't like Amber very much. And she didn't like not liking someone.

On her way back to her locker, Gem saw Amber. She tried to duck behind the water fountain before Amber saw her, but—too late! "Hey, Gem," said Amber. "I've been looking for you. You're one hard rock to dig up! We're all going out for ice cream. Do you want to come?"

Did she? Gem loved Rocky Road's Ice Cream Cave. And she knew all her friends would be there. But before she could stop herself, she was saying, "No, Amber. I can't. I've got to get home."

"OK, Gem," said Amber. "Maybe next time!"

"Maybe I *do* need to see the nurse," Gem thought. "Or maybe I'm just going crazy!"

When Gem got home, her dad was sitting at the kitchen table looking at the checkbook. "How's my little diamond?" he asked.

"Dad, do you think maybe I could get those new boots this weekend?"

"Sugar rock, we just don't have the money right now," her dad said.

"But it's not fair!" Gem cried.

"What's not fair, Gem? Why are you so sad?"

"Well," Gem began, "there's this new girl, Amber, and she has *everything.* Nice clothes, a sparkin' backpack, and the BEST boots!" Gem was beside herself. "And she took all our friends to Rocky Road's today!"

"Why didn't you go?" her dad asked.

"I just didn't feel like it. I don't know what's wrong with me, Dad. When I think about Amber, I feel awful all over."

"Gem, it sounds like you're a little jealous of Amber and the things she has."

"I'm not jealous!" Gem said. "Hmm. Maybe I am, a little. But I don't want to be!"

"When I get jealous of people, I play the gratitude game," her dad said.

"What's the gratitude game?" asked Gem.

"I just start to tell God all of the things I'm grateful for. When I think of all the ways God takes care of me, it's hard for me to be angry about what other people have."

"I don't know, Dad," said Gem. "But I'll give it a try."

Gem went to her room and thought about what a great, understanding dad she had. "Thank you God, for a dad who listens to me," she prayed. She went to her desk and got out her favorite journal. "Thank you, God, for a place to write my thoughts. And thanks for hearing me when I talk to you." She looked out her bedroom window. "Thank you, God, for my room, and the beautiful world outside of it." Suddenly she realized she didn't have a sick feeling in her stomach anymore. "Dad!" she called, "I'm going to Rocky Road's!"

Her dad smiled. "OK, sugar rock. Have a good time."

When she got there, Chip, Splinter, Carb, and all her other school friends where enjoying the best ice cream in town. "Hey, Amber," said Gem. "I hope it's OK that I came."

"OK?" said Amber. "It's terrific!"

"Yeah," said Gem. "Terrific!" And this time she meant it.

Thinkin' It Through!

* How do you feel when a friend has games or clothes or other things that you don't have?

* Why do you think the "gratitude game" made Gem feel better?

* "Covet" means to really want what belongs to someone else. Why do you think God commanded us not to covet?

TC TWINS TALK TEN

★ **COMMANDMENT 10:** Do not covet.

Sometimes commercials or other people can make us focus so much on wanting certain things that we start to think that *we* have to have them or we won't be happy. But is that really true?

God loves to give us gifts. In fact, James tells us, "Every good and perfect gift is from above, coming down from the Father" (James 1:17). But he doesn't want our desire for *things* to get in the way of our relationships with *people*—or with him. James says that "what causes fights and quarrels among you" is that "you want something but don't get it" (James 4:1, 2). It's hard to be kind or generous or encouraging to a friend when all you can think about is what they have that you want.

Sometimes jealousy is called the green-eyed monster. Jealousy can turn you into a monster, for sure! If you've ever been jealous of what someone has, you know what we mean. You feel sick in your stomach. It's hard to even say hello. And sometimes you can get mad at God, too. Why hasn't he given you what you want? Why did he give it to your friend? Does he like her better? You can think some crazy things when the green-eyed monster has a hold on you.

Try to think about it this way: God knows what he's doing. He's got a plan for you and your life, and he has given you the things you need to do what he wants you to do. If he's given other things to other people, he may have other plans for them. But his plan for you is perfect—and probably pretty exciting. So don't worry about what you *don't* have. Thank God for what you *do* have, and ask him how you can use it to help people learn more about him!

SET IN STONE: TC Twins Memory Verse

Godliness with contentment is great gain.

1 Timothy 6:6

GET ROCKIN'
HERE ARE SOME QUICK CURES FOR COVETING!

✸ Play the gratitude game that Gem's dad taught her. Think about what God has given you—and thank him for it!

✸ Give things away! Sounds like a crazy solution to coveting, doesn't it? But when people cheerfully share what they have with others, they usually enjoy everything else even more.

✸ Pray for the person you are jealous of. Ask God to help you show his love to that person. It's hard to resent someone you are praying for!

★ GOLD NUGGET GUIDES ★
www.godrocksvideo.com

GET ROCKIN'

STORIES FEATURING YOUR FAVORITE GOD ROCKS! CHARACTERS WITH NUGGETS OF WISDOM JUST FOR YOU FROM GOD ROCKS! HEROES.

★ ROCKIN' WITH THE RULES
Understanding the Ten Commandments

Who needs rules? We all do! Follow Chip and his friends as they learn to use God's rules to help them make good decisions in tough situations.

24241 *ISBN 0-7847-1127-5*

★ BEYOND A BLAST FROM THE PAST
Discovering why God made you

Are you ready for a cosmic discovery? God made all of creation with a purpose—including you! Join *The God Rocks!* as they find out what God's plan is all about.

24242 *ISBN 0-7847-1355-3*

★ MORE THAN A SPLATBALL GAME
Squaring off with the giants in your life

Have you ever stood nose-to-knee with trouble? We all have! Chip, Gem, Carb, and Splinter experience their share of giants and wind up victorious—and so can you!

24243 *ISBN 0-7847-1457-6*

THE HIPPEST NEW ANIMATED VIDEO SERIES ON THE BLOCK WITH LIFE LESSONS AND BIBLE TRUTHS!

IF ROCKS FROM BIBLE TIMES COULD TALK, WOULD THEY KEEP SILENT ABOUT THE AMAZING EVENTS THEY WITNESSED? NO WAY! THAT'S WHY EVERY GOD ROCKS! HERO HAS SOMETHING IMPORTANT TO SAY!

✳ **TEN ROCKIN' RULES** *or . . . Wakin' up is hard to do*
Chip and his friends learn from the Ten Commandment Twins that God gives us rules because he loves us. Join Chip, Gem, Carb, and Splinter on this wild ride full of twists and turns, and you'll wake up to discover Ten Rockin' Rules!
DVD includes an avalanche of extras: *Blooper gems, interviews with the creators and the band, God Rocks! desktop wallpaper, widescreen option and MORE!*

✳ **A BLAST FROM THE PAST** *or . . . Anybody got change for a Buck?*
Has Rocky Ridge been invaded by mutant vegetables from outer space? Join The God Rocks! as they unearth the solution to the alien mystery. Along the way, you'll hear from Buck, a traveling sales rock, who blasts onto the scene and realizes that God created the universe and everything in it with a purpose.
DVD includes a meteor shower of extras: *"This Is the Day" music video featuring The God Rocks!, "You've Been Searching" music video featuring Sheryl Stacey, samples from the debut music CD, widescreen option and MORE!*

✳ **SPLATBALL SQUARE-OFF** *or . . . Nose to knee with a defiant giant*
As the annual splatball championship begins, the Rocky Ridge Rangers are shaking in their shoes! But Bullseye (Mickey Rooney), their coach, is a God Rocks hero who has been face to face with Goliath, a very defiant giant. In the end, The God Rocks! find out that when we look to God, our giants are never as big as they seem.
DVD includes a ballpark full of extras: *The God Rocks! Cry Out tour highlights, interviews, games, and MORE!*

VHS 24214 UPC 7-07529-24214-9
DVD 24227 UPC 7-07529-24227-9

VHS 24215 UPC 7-07529-24215-6
DVD 24228 UPC 7-07529-24228-6

VHS 24216 UPC 7-07529-24216-3
DVD 24229 UPC 7-07529-24229-3

Cry Out

SPARKIN' MUSIC THAT'S ENERGIZING, POP-DRIVEN AND CREATED ESPECIALLY FOR KIDS WHO AREN'T AFRAID TO SHOUT "GOD ROCKS!"

★ CRY OUT

One great new kids' video series, four talented musicians and 14 hot-as-lava songs combine to introduce The God Rocks! in their debut music release, *Cry Out*. The CD features original 10-karat songs of praise and encouragement from the first three episodes of God Rocks! and MORE! Kids will want to sing along with this sparkin' new band as they praise God and give honor to him.

24261 UPC 7-07529-24261-3